STEM
ON THE BATTLEFIELD

SMOKE SCREENS AND GAS MASKS
CHEMISTRY GOES TO WAR

Tim Ripley

Lerner Publications ◆ Minneapolis

Lerner Publications Company
A division of Lerner Publishing Group, Inc.
241 First Avenue North
Minneapolis, MN 55401 USA

For reading levels and more information, look up this title at www.lernerbooks.com.

Main body text set in Verdana Regular 11/16.5.
Typeface provided by Microsoft.

Picture Credits:
Front Cover: ©Ryan J. Lane/Getty Images,
Interior: ©Ryan J. Lane/Getty Images, Front Cover; ©Robert Hunt Library, 1; ©Robert Hunt Library, 4; ©Robert Hunt Library, 5; ©Sergey Kamshylin/Shutterstock, 6; ©Department of Defense, 7; ©iStock/Thinkstock, 8; ©Samuel Scott, 9; ©North Wind Picture Archives/Alamy, 10; ©Robert Hunt Library, 11; ©Robert Hunt Library, 12; ©ArtiMax/Shutterstock, 13; Iurapex/Shutterstock, 14; ©Robert Hunt Library, 15; ©Robert Hunt Library, 16; ©Robert Hunt Library, 17tr; ©Veleknez/Shutterstock, 17br; ©Jurand/Shutterstock, 18; ©ADA_photo/Shutterstock, 19; ©iStock/Thinkstock, 20; ©Robert Hunt Library, 21tr; ©Studio37/Shutterstock, 21br; ©Robert Hunt Library, 22; ©Department of Defense, 23; ©Everett Historical/Shutterstock, 24; ©Everett Historical/Shutterstock, 25tl; ©Robert Hunt Library, 25cr; ©Robert Hunt Library, 26; ©Robert Hunt Library, 27; ©Robert Hunt Library, 28; ©Robert Hunt Library, 29; ©Everett Historical/Shutterstock, 30; ©National Archives, 31; ©National Archives, 32; ©Robert Hunt Library, 33; ©Robert Hunt Library, 34; ©Department of Defense, 35; ©National Archives, 36; ©ZUMA Press/Alamy, 37; ©Robert Hunt Library, 38; ©Robert Hunt Library, 39tr; ©National Archives, 39b; ©Valery Sibrikov, 40; ©Chemical Heritage Foundation, 41tr; ©Department of Defense, 41br; ©Department of Defense, 42; ©Department of Defense, 43.

Brown Bear Books has made every attempt to contact the copyright holder.
If you have any information please contact licensing@brownbearbooks.co.uk

Library of Congress Cataloging-in-Publication Data

Names: Ripley, Tim, author.
Title: Smoke screens and gas masks : chemistry goes to war / Tim Ripley.
Other titles: Chemistry goes to war
Description: Minneapolis : Lerner Publications, [2017] | Series: STEM on the battlefield | Includes index. | Audience: Grades 4–6. | Audience: Ages 9–12.
Identifiers: LCCN 2016055032 (print) | LCCN 2016055325 (ebook) | ISBN 9781512439250 (lb : alk. paper) | ISBN 9781512449532 (eb pdf)
Subjects: LCSH: Military art and science—History—Juvenile literature. | Chemistry—History—Juvenile literature. | Military weapons—History—Juvenile literature.
Classification: LCC U27 .R55 2017 (print) | LCC U27 (ebook) | DDC 355/.07—dc23

LC record available at https://lccn.loc.gov/2016055032

Manufactured in the United States of America
1-42138-25411-3/20/2017

CONTENTS

CHEMISTRY AT WAR

During World War I (1914–1918), German commanders wanted to capture a French fortress at Verdun, on France's eastern border. On February 21, 1916, German **artillery** opened fire. In just under five hours, 800 big guns fired around one million **shells** at French positions. The French defended the fort for nine more months before the Germans withdrew. Despite its failure, the **bombardment** was one of the biggest ever fired, and it showed the importance of chemistry in warfare. Chemists had not only developed explosives for the shells. They had also figured out ways to make millions of shells quickly and relatively safely.

British workers make shells in a factory during World War I.

WEAPONS DEVELOPMENT

Chemistry is the science of the substances that make up all matter. Chemists examine how substances react to forces. They also combine substances to make new ones.

Chemistry has shaped weapons since ancient times. Ancient peoples learned how to make metal blades and points for weapons. Next came the discovery of gunpowder in ancient China. When gunpowder reached Europe in the thirteenth century, it transformed warfare. Gunpowder allowed for the development of weapons such as cannons, pistols, and **muskets**. In the eighteenth and nineteenth centuries, chemists developed new explosives and ammunition. They came up with weapons such as poison gas and **incendiary** weapons to cause fires. Chemists also created new materials to protect soldiers in battle. In the twenty-first century, chemistry remains at the heart of warfare.

SWORDS AND BLADES

One of the first uses of chemistry in warfare was to make bladed weapons. The process depended on being able to heat and shape metals.

The earliest weapons were made from stone or **flint**. In the fourth millennium BCE, people learned to forge bronze. They used the new metal to make sharper blades for weapons. The stronger bronze blades and arrowheads gave armies an advantage.

Ancient peoples such as Egyptians supplied their armies with bronze swords and axes, as well as spears and arrows. Bronze was quite soft, however. Over time, bronze blades bent or grew dull.

In about 1300 BCE, people learned to achieve very high temperatures in furnaces. That allowed them to extract iron from iron **ore**.

Early chemists learned to melt metals at very high temperatures. Liquid metals could be poured into molds.

A US Marine fits a bayonet to his weapon. Steel bayonets are still used for hand-to-hand fighting.

This developmment marked the start of the Iron Age. People soon began to use iron to make weapons.

IRON AND STEEL

Iron made bronze **obsolete**. Bronze weapons could not pierce iron armor. In turn, iron was replaced by steel by around the 300s BCE. Steel was even stronger, and lighter, than iron. It also kept its sharp edge for longer.

In the modern era, **infantry** soldiers still attach steel bayonets to their rifles. Bayonets are used as stabbing weapons in close combat.

Metallurgy and Metals

Bronze is an alloy, a metal made by mixing two or more metals. Bronze is made by mixing copper with tin. Metallurgy is the science of combining metals to make alloys. Early chemists learned to use heat to create new metals. The new alloys were stronger, lighter, and easier to make into weapons than pure metals had been.

FIRE AS A WEAPON

Since prehistoric times, fire has been an important weapon. Early chemists learned to direct fire against targets.

Ancient armies used fire as a destructive weapon. Many early battles were sieges. In a siege, an army surrounded a walled city to force it to surrender. Fire could help burn wooden city walls and create gaps for soldiers to enter the city. Burning **missiles** were also thrown into besieged towns. The missiles set fire to buildings. That terrified people inside the towns.

Wooden defenses and buildings burned easily. Medieval buildings stood close together, so fires spread quickly.

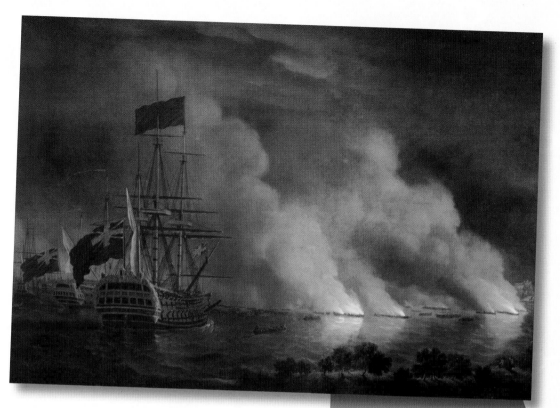

FIRE AND WATER

The first incendiary weapons were burning bundles of hay or grass. They were fired with catapults and bows. At sea, incendiary weapons were used to set fire to enemy warships. Ships would sink or be put out of action. Sailors filled old ships with fuel. They set the fuel on fire and pushed the fire ships toward enemy ships.

French rafts full of burning materials float toward ships of the British navy in 1759. France and Britain were fighting over control of the French colony in Canada.

Early incendiary weapons could easily be put out with water, and they could not be used in the rain. They were also difficult and dangerous to move and use.

Greek Fire

Greek fire was a flammable gel that could be molded into balls and fired. Its exact composition is unknown, but it was invented during the Byzantine Empire. The Byzantines fought their Muslim neighbors from the seventh to the thirteenth centuries. They fired the weapon from catapults or attached it to arrows to fight off their attackers.

GREEK FIRE

In the seventh century, early incendiary missiles were replaced by Greek fire. This was a sticky **flammable** material. It burned even on the surface of water. That made it useful for naval and siege warfare.

This weapon, called a trebuchet, used a long lever to throw barrels of Greek fire toward the enemy.

Sailors used Greek fire to make burning missiles. They threw the missiles from catapults on the decks of ships. This helped them to bombard enemy ships from a safe distance.

Greek fire was used in weapons such as cannons. These weapons often burned down wooden fortifications in sieges. Then engineers began to build city walls out of stone, and they replaced the straw roofs of castles with tiled roofs. Tiled roofs were far more difficult to set on fire.

The First Flamethrowers

Byzantine warships carried the world's first flamethrowers. A simple pump was fitted to the front of a ship. Sailors pumped to build up pressure, then used the pressure to shoot a devastating stream of Greek fire.

This illustration from the twelfth century shows Byzantine sailors using a flamethrower against an enemy vessel.

THE FIRST EXPLOSIVES

In the thirteenth century, Europeans heard stories about a magical potion in China. It was said that the potion could create explosions.

Gunpowder was probably invented in China sometime in the ninth century. Experts think that Chinese scientists wanted to set targets such as enemy buildings on fire. They were trying to create an incendiary weapon like Greek fire. The scientists probably mixed two chemicals called sulfur and saltpeter. The mixture did not just burn. It exploded. The early chemists probably did more experiments. They figured out the right amounts of sulfur and saltpeter to use to get the biggest explosion. This new mixture was gunpowder.

Chinese archers use special baskets to launch burning arrows in this illustration from the eleventh century. Each launcher can fire multiple arrows.

THE FIRST ROCKETS

Gunpowder weapons evolved quickly. The next step was the creation of the first rockets. They resembled large exploding arrows, or modern fireworks. Then Chinese scientists figured out how to make the first cannons. They realized that an explosion in a small space would cause a rapid burst of gas. If that gas was contained, it could push a **projectile** along a barrel at high speed.

Chinese Gunpowder

Chinese gunpowder was a mixture of sulfur and saltpeter. It was only explosive if the right quantities were used. Gunpowder was also called black powder because of its color. It changed warfare completely. Gunpowder led to the development of exploding missiles. It also led to weapons that could fire bullets or shells over long distances.

A Chinese soldier uses a burning stick to set light to an exploding rocket. The first gunpowder weapons were like modern fireworks.

13

If the speed was high enough, the projectile would keep traveling forward after it had left the barrel and the gas had **dispersed**. This is the concept behind the operation of all cannons and guns.

The earliest Chinese cannons were small. Later cannons were much bigger. They could fire projectiles hundreds of yards. The first cannon barrels were made from wood. They sometimes split because of the huge forces generated by the explosions inside. Wooden barrels were soon replaced by barrels made from cast metal. The first cannon balls were made of metal or stone. They were later hollowed out and filled with explosives, so the balls shattered on impact. This caused damage over a greater area.

Early cannons defended the Great Wall of China. China's rulers built the long wall to protect their empire from peoples who lived to the north.

Many battles in China were sieges of castles or cities. Gunpowder weapons made it far more difficult to build defenses against attack.

FIRST FIREARMS

Chinese scientists next developed the first firearms. These were the first gunpowder weapons to be used by individuals. They were long-barreled guns that were carried and fired by individual soldiers. The guns were clumsy to use and were also unreliable. Often, the soldier missed the target or the gun failed to fire. However, these first firearms pointed the way for future weapons development in Europe.

Explosives and Castles

Gunpowder transformed siege warfare in China. Attackers used catapults or rockets to fire bombs at fortress walls. Castles or cities could no longer be easily defended. Explosives could knock holes in high walls, so new fortifications were built with walls filled with rock and soil. These materials absorbed explosions without collapsing.

GUNPOWDER IN EUROPE

Gunpowder reached Europe in the middle of the thirteenth century. Chemists figured out ways to make the new invention. Engineers came up with new weapons to use it.

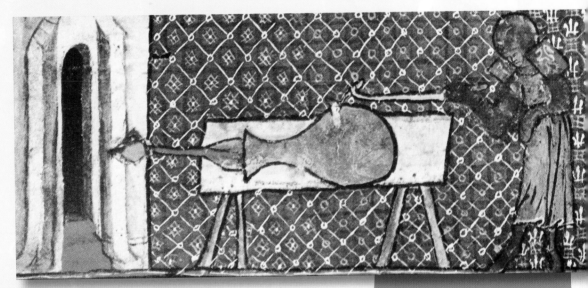

An illustration from 1326 shows a European soldier lighting the fuse of an early cannon. The cannon is loaded with an arrow-like missile.

Chemists made gunpowder from sulfur, charcoal, and potassium or saltpeter. The first gunpowder weapons used a spark to **ignite** the gunpowder. The gunpowder created an explosive flash and a shockwave that damaged anything nearby. It also set fire to flammable materials.

Engineers realized that gunpowder could be ignited in a tight space to fire a missile. They began making cannons, pistols, and muskets.

The weapons fired shells, bullets, or rockets. By the fifteenth century, every army in Europe used gunpowder weapons.

VITAL MATERIALS

The ingredients of gunpowder became vital items for armies. Countries such as Britain and France had large empires. They could get the materials from overseas. That helped them manufacture more gunpowder. Countries also wanted to make metal cannons and guns. This need to make weapons helped start the Industrial Revolution. This was a period of industrial change that began in the mid-1700s.

Modern battle reenactors fire a light cannon. In the 1700s, armies began using light cannons that were easy to move and could be fired by a small gun crew.

17

SMOKELESS POWDER

Gunpowder caused a problem on the battlefield. It produced thick clouds of smoke, making it impossible for commanders to see what was happening.

The first gunpowder small arms were arquebuses. These are sometimes called muskets. They were loaded by tipping gunpowder and a bullet into the end of the barrel. The weapon was fired with a burning fuse that set off the gunpowder. By the late nineteenth century, muzzle-loading muskets had been replaced by breech-loaders. In these, bullets were loaded at the back of the barrel with a **percussion** cap behind.

Battlefield Visibility

From the seventeenth century to the early nineteenth century, soldiers often wore brightly colored uniforms. This helped their commanders to see them during battle. During this time, soldiers fired their muskets all at once. The battlefield became engulfed in clouds of gunpowder smoke, making it difficult to see.

Smoke rises as modern battlefield reenactors fire muskets from the early 1800s. The thick smoke hung in the air and burned the eyes and nose.

When the trigger was pulled, a hammer struck the bullet. This set off the smokeless powder in the percussion cap.

EXPLOSIVE BULLETS

Breech-loaders used new smokeless explosives developed by chemists in Europe and North America. These explosives were more powerful than gunpowder.

For the first time, bullets or artillery missiles could be combined with an explosive. The **warhead** and the **propellant** were in a single metal container. This was like a modern bullet or shell. The firing pin of a rifle struck the sparking cap behind the bullet. With this development, weapons could be safely transported and stored, and the mass production of ammunition became possible.

Modern rifle shells include a percussion cap at the back, an explosive powder, and the bullet itself at the tip.

NEW EXPLOSIVES

In the nineteenth century, chemists developed new types of explosives. The new explosives could be used to make large amounts of ammunition.

In the middle of the nineteenth century, the Italian chemist Ascanio Sobrero invented a liquid explosive. It was named nitroglycerin. The explosive was powerful, but it was unstable, meaning it could go off if it was accidently dropped or if it became too hot. Nitroglycerin caused many accidents. It even blew up factories where it was made.

Nitroglycerin came in sticks for easy handling. The explosives were set off by a fuse attached to a generator (left) that was used to create an electrical spark.

DYNAMITE

One accidental explosion of nitroglycerin in 1864 destroyed an arms factory owned by the Nobel family in Sweden. The younger brother of the chemist Alfred Nobel was killed. Nobel figured out a way to mix nitroglycerin with other materials to make it more stable. He came up with a solid form of explosive that he called dynamite. Nobel registered, or patented, dynamite as a new invention in 1867. Dynamite was safe to handle. Unlike nitroglycerin, it could be pushed into small spaces to produce maximum power.

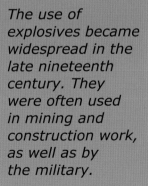

The use of explosives became widespread in the late nineteenth century. They were often used in mining and construction work, as well as by the military.

This painting shows German shells being fired at British warships in the Battle of Jutland, fought in 1916 during World War I.

A POWERFUL EXPLOSIVE

Meanwhile, in 1863 the German scientist Julius Wilbrand invented trinitrotoluene, or TNT. TNT was one of the most powerful explosives of the time. It was also the first explosive that could safely be turned into a liquid. The liquid could be poured into shells during the manufacturing process.

TNT transformed naval warfare in World War I. German manufacturers used TNT to make armor-piercing shells. The tip of the shell could pierce a hole in the armor of an enemy ship. Then the shell could pass through the hole into the ship. A delayed-action fuse set off the shell's TNT load, causing huge amounts of damage.

PLASTIC EXPLOSIVE

In 1875, Alfred Nobel invented something that he called gelignite. Gelignite was the first plastic explosive. The chemical looked like modeling clay. It was soft enough to be molded into shape by hand and was more powerful than dynamite. It was also very stable. It would only explode when it was triggered with a special detonator.

A US airman pushes plastic explosive into the tip of a captured enemy shell in Iraq in the 2000s. He will detonate the explosive to destroy the shell safely.

Plastic Explosives

Plastic explosives are solid explosives. The explosive can be molded into any shape or size. That makes it popular for demolition work. Different shaped charges can be placed precisely where they are required.

POISONOUS GAS

Chemists invented poison gas during World War I. They hoped the new weapon would provide a breakthrough in trench warfare.

The British and French on one side and the Germans on the other had dug rows of trenches facing one another. The conflict was at a **stalemate**. Germany had an advanced chemical industry. German military leaders asked chemists to come up with a new weapon. They wanted to be able to kill enemy soldiers in their trenches. Other weapons were not able to harm French and British soldiers who had taken cover there.

Clouds of poison gas drift across trenches in a training exercise. This photograph was taken from an airplane in northern France.

The US Army Engineer Corps took this photograph. The action was staged. The Army wanted to warn soldiers about the effects of a poison gas attack.

CHLORINE GAS

The German chemists came up with poisonous gas. Chlorine gas was used in manufacturing, so chemists already knew it could cause choking and even death. Chemical factories could easily manufacture the gas in large quantities. The challenge was to figure out how to get the gas into enemy trenches.

The first poison gas was used in 1915. It was simply released from large metal containers in the German trenches.

THE BRAINS

Fritz Haber

(1868–1934) was a German chemist who had won the Nobel Prize for chemistry. He was the obvious choice to lead the effort to use chlorine gas as a weapon. He oversaw creation of the gas. He also worked to develop a new delivery system. Haber took the first gas weapons to France. He used them in action for the first time in May 1915.

Gas in the Trenches

Chlorine gas was easy to see and smell. In late 1915 French chemists developed phosgene gas. It had no color and had little odor. Soldiers had no time to protect themselves against it. Mustard gas, another type of gas, was heavy and formed an oily substance on the ground.

The chlorine gas caused many deaths. It also spread terror among enemy troops. But relying on the wind had many disadvantages. There was always a danger that the gas would blow back toward German lines.

GAS SHELLS

After the first German gas attacks, the British and French responded by making their own gas weapons.

British soldiers wearing gas masks take shelter in a trench while gas fills the air around them.

These British soldiers were wounded in a gas attack in 1918. Many have bandages on their damaged eyes. Each man holds the shoulder of the man in front because they cannot see where they are going.

The two sides raced to make gas a more effective weapon. One result was the creation of gas shells. These shells were fired from artillery. They fell deep behind enemy lines and created huge clouds of gas. The gas blew all over enemy positions.

The Germans, the British, and the French all experimented with new types of gas. The most deadly was mustard gas. It acted as a blister agent. It caused deep and painful burns to a victim's skin or lungs.

GAS MASKS

In World War I, scientists developed ways to protect soldiers from gas attacks. Modern gas masks use similar technology against illegal gas attacks.

Chemists figured out a way to stop the effects of chlorine gas. Soldiers needed to cover their noses and mouths with **gauze** or cotton so they would not breathe in the gas. They soaked these materials in a solution of a chemical called bicarbonate. The bicarbonate helped to prevent the effects of chlorine gas. Bicarbonate was rushed to the trenches in large quantities.

Scottish soldiers wear pads of gauze over their mouths as protection against gas. Goggles protect their eyes.

When phosgene was developed, soldiers wore plastic hoods with slits for the eyes. The next gas masks were made from fabric. They had glass goggles sewn in and an air filter to protect the wearer's mouth and nose. Soldiers kept birds in cages to warn them of a gas attack. The birds died quickly if there was gas in the air.

PROTECTIVE CLOTHING

Mustard gas burned the skin. It did not have to be breathed in to cause harm. As protection, soldiers wore heavy gas-resistant capes, suits, and pants. Mustard gas lingered in the bottom of trenches. Once an area was **contaminated**, it had to be avoided.

World War I ended in 1918. In 1925 the use of poisonous gas was banned under an international treaty named the Geneva Protocol. The treaty was signed by 140 countries.

Animal Gas Masks

In World War I, armies used horses and mules to pull supply wagons and field guns. These animals also suffered from the effects of poison gas, so special gas masks were designed for animals. The masks slipped over the animals' heads and had clear plastic goggles that allowed them to see.

These German soldiers have fitted a gas mask over the nose of their donkey. Later, special gas masks were designed for animals.

INCENDIARY DEVICES

In the early decades of the twentieth century, developments in science had a major effect on air warfare.

One key development was the production of material that was highly combustible, meaning that it caught fire easily. This material was placed inside the tips of bullets. This created incendiary bullets that started fires.

Incendiary bullets were first used by pilots from Britain, the United States, and their **allies** in World War I to shoot down German Zeppelins, or **airships**. The huge airships were filled with flammable gases that blew up easily.

A German Zeppelin burns in this illustration of an attack by a British airplane. Incendiary bullets set fire to the gas inside the airship.

A white phosphorus bomb explodes during the Vietnam War (1955–1975). US bombers used the bombs to clear jungles where the enemy could hide.

Incendiary bullets were later used in the machine guns of airplanes. Warplanes at the time had wooden frames. Their outer skins were made of material such as canvas. These materials were flammable, so pilots tried to set enemy aircraft on fire.

SPREADING FIRE

Incendiary technology was also used in sea and land warfare. Using small incendiary ammunition and hand guns, it became possible to set enemy ships or vehicles on fire.

White Phosphorus

White phosphorus burns at a very high temperature. It can set fire to cloth, fuel, or ammunition. When it burns, white phosphorus also creates large clouds of smoke. It was used during World War II (1939–1945) to create smoke screens. The smoke hid troops or ships from the enemy. US forces also used phosphorus in the Vietnam War to set fire to the hiding places of the enemy.

Weapons makers also discovered new uses for incendiary weapons. Not all incendiary weapons are used to set targets on fire. Some light fires near targets. This marks the targets for other attackers. Incendiary weapons also produce smoke. The smoke hides friendly troops or locations.

VISIBLE BULLETS

Some incendiary bullets burn as they travel through the air. This means they can be seen in flight, which allows friendly forces to avoid danger. This is important for aircrews carrying out raids.

An airplane drops a phosphorus bomb above a disused warship during US Navy tests of incendiary weapons in 1921. The ship was eventually sunk.

Lines made by tracer bullets light up the sky above a US airfield on the island of Okinawa in 1945, during the Pacific War with Japan.

Sometimes pilots and aircrew cannot hear what is happening outside their own aircraft. Incendiary bullets show them if any other planes are firing.

MODERN BOMBS

Modern incendiary bombs use chemicals that ignite fuel, ammunition, or even foliage. They can be used to burn away vegetation to reveal any enemy positions hidden by trees or undergrowth.

Tracer Shells

Tracer shells or bullets can be seen with the naked eye. As a weapon fires, it lights a chemical at the back of the shell or bullet. The chemical burns as it flies through the air. Its path is visible as a streak of color. This helps those firing the weapon to make sure their shot is on target.

FLAMETHROWERS

A modern version of Greek fire was widely used in World War I. It killed enemy soldiers inside bunkers and other fortifications.

German engineers developed a flamethrower that was used for the first time in February 1915. The device sprayed out a jet of liquid fuel, like Greek fire. The jet was then ignited. The burning fuel could be aimed into narrow firing slits in **bunkers**. A trigger allowed the operator to fire in short bursts. The first flamethrowers were difficult to move. The next version of the weapon had a fuel tank. It could be carried on a soldier's back. These weapons were used in attacks on enemy strongholds.

US tanks use flamethrowers to clear a hillside during the invasion of Okinawa in 1945.

But the weapons had a limited range. They could not carry much fuel and were unreliable. If enemy fire struck the fuel tank, it would explode, and the soldier carrying it would likely die.

BIGGER WEAPONS

In World War II, flamethrowers were mounted on tanks and armored vehicles. They carried more fuel. They could shoot their jets of flame farther. Flamethrowers on armored vehicles were also safer to operate.

THE BRAINS

Richard Fiedlar was a German scientist who designed the first modern flamethrower. The weapon was small, light to carry, and could shoot flame about 20 yards (18 meters). The weapon was first used in 1911. Later, all flamethrowers were based on Fiedlar's original design.

A US Marine uses a modern flamethrower to clear vegetation.

SMOKE SCREENS

Smoke is an effective way to hide troop movements on the battlefield. It can be generated from different chemicals.

In World War I, both sides had machine guns and artillery facing the enemy trenches. Chemists tried to develop smoke screens. They wanted to hide troops moving between the trenches. The first smoke screens burned wood or fuel oil to create smoke. But these screens were not easy to control. It was also difficult to keep the fires from going out.

US soldiers create a smoke screen during World War II.

So scientists tried creating smoke screens using mixtures of chemicals. The chemicals reacted to give off thick clouds of smoke. During World War I, commanders used smoke screens to shield troop movements. They let off smoke as they gathered large numbers of soldiers ready for an attack on the enemy trenches.

SMUDGE POTS

In later conflicts, chemists developed smudge pots. These containers of oil had small wicks at the top. The wicks were lit to create smoke to hide targets from air **surveillance** and attack. The Germans used smudge pots in World War II. The Vietnamese also used them in the Vietnam War in the 1960s. Vietnamese fighters were trying to prevent US bombers from finding their targets. The same technique was used by Iraqi troops during the US-led invasion of 2003.

Smudge pots held a fuel such as oil. They burned slowly, generating huge amounts of smoke.

THE BRAINS

Alonzo Patterson

Alonzo Patterson was a smuggler in New Orleans in the 1920s. Under Prohibition, alcohol was banned. Patterson smuggled it into the United States from abroad. He used smoke screens to hide his ships from law enforcement officials. In World War II, Patterson helped the US Navy develop better smoke screens.

Napalm is a combination of gasoline and a thickening agent. It creates a burning gel that sticks to plants, buildings, or people.

The name *napalm* comes from the chemicals used to make the thickening agent. These are aluminum salts of naphthenic and palmitic acids. Napalm cannot be easily removed or washed off. If victims survive the initial attack, their wounds continue to burn for several days. Napalm was developed during World War II. It was mainly used in Asia to burn away thick jungles to find out if Japanese soldiers were hiding there.

US bombers drop napalm in the Philippines in World War II. The napalm cleared the jungle hiding enemy soldiers.

Napalm bombs were set off in the air. The burning gel spread across a wide area. These bombs were also used by US bombers in Japan. They helped set fire to the wooden buildings in Japanese cities.

KOREA AND VIETNAM

After World War II, napalm was used in the Korean War (1950–1953). US forces used it to stop Chinese infantry. In the Vietnam War, US forces used napalm to burn away jungle vegetation. The jungle was a common hiding place of enemy **guerrillas**. When US aircraft bombed civilians by accident, napalm caused horrific injuries. The use of napalm became **controversial**.

A napalm bomb explodes in a fireball behind a US patrol during the Vietnam War.

MODERN ARMOR

Steel has been vital in warfare since the days of medieval knights in armor. But steel is very heavy. This is a drawback on the battlefield. Scientists have found different ways to create modern armor.

In the late Middle Ages, firearms replaced bows and arrows. Armor became less useful. In order to protect the wearer against musket balls, steel armor had to be very thick. Armor became very heavy. Knights were no longer able to move around easily when they wore it. Steel armor quickly disappeared from the battlefield. It did not appear again for several centuries.

VEHICLES AND SHIPS

In modern warfare, steel has also been used to protect vehicles and ships. The first steel-hulled battleships appeared in the 1860s.

Steel armor protected the body from swords but could not withstand the impact of a musket ball traveling at a high speed.

The steel tank appeared in 1916. Toward the end of the twentieth century, however, new weapons made steel obsolete. High Explosive Anti-Tank (HEAT) warheads created super-hot jets of **molten** metal when they struck a target. These jets punched through steel by melting it.

Early in the twenty-first century, scientists came up with new ways to protect vehicles. They made armor from layers of plastic or a material called a **polymer**.

THE BRAINS

Stephanie Kwolek
(1923–2014)
Stephanie Kwolek was a US chemist. She worked for the DuPont chemical company developing synthetic fibers. She played a key role in developing Kevlar in 1965. Kevlar was the first of the new generation of superstrong materials. It began to transform battlefield armor in the 1970s.

A US soldier uses a weapon called a bazooka to fire HEAT missiles during training in the 2000s. The missiles penetrate steel armor on vehicles.

Bullet-Proof Armor

Superstrong fibers such as Kevlar began to appear in the 1960s. They could be woven into bullet-proof vests, seats, vehicle panels, or helmets. The fibers provided much better protection from bullets than steel armor. Woven materials absorb impact without the fibers breaking apart.

The new polymer armor was toughened so that it would be able to resist HEAT warheads. The plastic changes the chemistry of HEAT jets and cools them down so they cause less damage.

Superstrong plastics or polymers are also used in modern aircraft. Plastic panels are lightweight replacements for heavy metal. **Radar** fitted inside plastic aircraft also works more efficiently. Steel aircraft bodies, or fuselages, sometimes interfere with radar signals.

*This US soldier in Iraq in 2008 wears an Improved Outer Tactical Vest (IOTV). The vest has **ceramic** plates inside.*

MODERN MATERIALS

Lighter and stronger materials have also enabled the development of more effective protection for individual soldiers. In place of steel armor, soldiers now wear body armor made from modern materials. These materials include Kevlar, a superstrong fiber. Kevlar is used to make bullet-proof vests. These vests sometimes include plates made of metal or a super-hard ceramic material. The ceramic material shatters when it is hit by a bullet, and absorbs the energy of the impact.

Ceramic armor could not have been imagined even a few decades ago. Who knows what new materials chemists might come up with for use on the battlefields of the future?

Plastic materials help to make the US F-22 Raptor difficult for radar to detect. The airplane gives off a smaller radar signal than a bumble bee.

TIMELINE

c. 4000 BCE   Humans begin to use metal to make daggers and swords.

c. 1800 BCE   People learn how to generate high enough temperatures to melt iron from its ore.

c. 300 BCE   People learn to make steel, which they turn into stronger, lighter weapons.

600s   Byzantines use Greek fire, a burning gel that can be shot from an early flamethrower.

800s   Unknown Chinese chemists learn to make gunpowder.

c. 1250   Gunpowder appears for the first time in Europe.

c. 1500   Europe's armies start to use gunpowder weapons.

1610   The flintlock becomes the standard firing mechanism for the musket gun.

1867   Alfred Nobel invents dynamite.

1875   Nobel invents gelignite, the first plastic explosive.

1901   Richard Fiedlar suggests that the German army make a flamethrower. The first flamethrower appears in 1911.

1914	World War I breaks out in Europe. Pilots use incendiary bullets to destroy German airships, called Zeppelins.
1915	The Germans use poisonous gas for the first time, during World War I.
	The Germans carry out the biggest bombardment of the war, at Verdun.
1916	Allied engineers build the first tank.
1925	The use of poison gas in battle is banned by the Geneva Protocol.
1965	Chemist Stephanie Kwolek invents Kevlar, which is used in modern bulletproof vests.
1980	Iraq goes to war with its neighbor, Iran. The conflict lasts until 1988. Both sides make chemical weapons, which are against international law. Iraq uses its chemical weapons to attack Iran.
1993	An international agreement bans the manufacture or storage of all chemical weapons.
2013	The Syrian government uses the gas sarin to kill its own citizens who are protesting against government policies.
2014	US specialists destroy Syria's chemical weapons.

GLOSSARY

airships: long, thin balloons powered by engines

allies: countries that agree to work together for a particular purpose

artillery: large guns such as cannons

bombardment: a continuous attack with bombs or shells

bunkers: reinforced concrete shelters that are often underground

ceramic: made from hardened clay

contaminated: poisoned by contact with a poisonous substance

controversial: describes something that causes disagreement

dispersed: thinned out and disappeared

flammable: easily set on fire

flint: a hard rock that splits into flat sheets

gauze: a thin, transparent fabric

guerrillas: small groups of fighters who use tactics such as ambushes

ignite: to set fire to something

incendiary: intended to start a fire

infantry: soldiers who fight on foot

missiles: weapons that are propelled toward a target

molten: melted

muskets: long-barreled guns that are fired from the shoulder

obsolete: out of date

ore: rocks containing metals

percussion: describes something that is activated by being struck

polymer: an artifical material such as plastic

projectile: a missile fired from a gun

propellant: a substance that propels a rocket or fires a bullet

radar: a system for locating objects by using radio waves

shells: explosive artillery missiles

stalemate: a situation in which neither side in a conflict can win or take any action

surveillance: close observation of the enemy

warhead: the explosive head of a missile or shell

FURTHER RESOURCES

Books

Oxlade, Chris. *Inside Tanks and Heavy Artillery.* Minneapolis: Hungry Tomato, 2018.

Regan, Lisa. *Chemistry Is Explosive.* New York: Gareth Stevens Publishing, 2017.

Samuels, Charlie. *Machines and Weaponry of World War I.* New York: Gareth Stevens Publishing, 2013.

Wood, Alix. *Chemical Weapons.* New York: PowerKids Press, 2016.

Websites

Alfred Nobel
http://www.bbc.co.uk/history /historic_figures/nobel_alfred .shtml

Gunpowder from China
http://quatr.us/war /gunpowder.htm

The History of Explosives
http://inventors.about.com/od /estartinventions/a/explosives .htm

Stephanie Kwolek
http://www.women-inventors .com/Stephanie-Kwolek.asp

When Chemicals became Weapons of War
http://chemicalweapons .cenmag.org/when-chemicals -became-weapons-of-war/

INDEX